Tipton Po
Edit(

Tipton Poetry Journal, located in the heartland of the Midwest, publishes quality poetry from Indiana and around the world.

This issue features 47 poets from the United States (19 different states) and 5 poets from Australia, India and Morocco.

Beginning with this issue, we are choosing a Featured Poem for each issue with an award of $25. The featured poem was chosen by the Board of Directors of Brick Street Poetry, Inc., the Indiana non-profit organization who publishes *Tipton Poetry Journal.* Our Summer 2020 Featured Poem is "Odes to Satan" written by William Doreski. This poem can be found on page 8.

Cover Photo: "Summer Butterfly" by Barry Harris.

Print versions of *Tipton Poetry Journal* are available for purchase through amazon.com.

Barry Harris, Editor

Copyright 2020 by the Tipton Poetry Journal.

All rights remain the exclusive property of the individual contributors and may not be used without their permission.

Tipton Poetry Journal is published by Brick Street Poetry Inc., a tax-exempt non-profit organization under IRS Code 501(c)(3). Brick Street Poetry Inc. publishes the Tipton Poetry Journal, hosts the monthly poetry series *Poetry on Brick Street* and sponsors other poetry-related events.

Contents

Joan Colby 1
Karla Linn Merrifield 4
Gene Twaronite 5
Timothy Robbins 6
Christian Lozada 7
William Doreski 8
Charles Grosel 10
Shelby Stephenson 11
Samantha Fain 12
Richard Krohn 14
Mihika Jain 15
David Flynn 16
Rodney Torreson 18
Gilbert Allen 19
Sheila Wellehan 20
David M. Alper 21
Janet Reed 22
D.C. Buschmann 24
Laura Saint Martin 25
Daniel E. Blackston 25
Anne Whitehouse 26
Kelly Whiddon 26
Lorne Mook 28
Maree Reedman 28
Denise Thompson-Slaughter 30
R. Nikolas Macioci 31
Bruce Levine 32

Michael Estabrook	*32*
Jennifer McClellan	*34*
Brooke Dwojak Lehmann	*35*
Kit Kennedy	*36*
Tim Hawkins	*36*
Ryan David Leack	*38*
David Spicer	*40*
Doris Lynch	*42*
M. Ait Ali	*43*
Ann Boaden	*44*
Tom C. Hunley	*46*
John Stenberg	*47*
Michael Keshigian	*48*
Sandeep Kumar Mishra	*50*
Eugene Stevenson	*52*
J.T. Whitehead	*52*
Elizabeth Kidwell	*54*
Karen L. George	*55*
Mary Sexson	*56*
Fred D. White	*57*
Review: Library of My Hands by Joseph Heithaus	*58*
Contributor Biographies	*63*

Pandemic
Joan Colby

Darkness infests the trees.
The metaphor is virus,
How it settles invisibly
As light is slowly winched
Out of the world.

On the lakeshore, children
Kick a soccer ball. A group of women
Slide past practicing yoga moves.
Cyclists yell "heads-up", wheels whirring.
By morning, yellow tape closes
The possibilities of play.

How quickly this happened. A cold, a dry cough,
A tightness in the chest and suddenly: death.
Respirators hiss in isolated rooms. Only the stricken
Are admitted. Shelter-in-place: the new world order.

People fight over bread and mik,
Toilet paper, paper towels. First the old are taken,
Soon the young. Their fevered eyes
Pleading while others hide.

Black Death, Sweating Sickness, TB,
Spanish Flu, Ebola, HIV, now this.
We keep our distance.
Who remembers touching?

Corona Virus Redux
Joan Colby

Under the microscope the virus is beautiful.
Opening its petals like a crimson flower.
Unique as the century plant that blooms
So rarely, a graveyard scent warns
Of its emergence. Bats are suspect as the reservoir
Of the virus. Their wolf faces. The masks
To protect our breath. The virus
Is attracted to the lungs that wave
Like undersea plants. That listen
With giant ears. The song of the virus:
A woman with her hair braided into a corona
Of white flowers. A femme fatale is what
Every man wants: that danger, that little death.
Let each mouth open to another: the virus
Slides along the tongue and comes to rest.

Parson of Darkness
Joan Colby

He stands
At the door of his church
Vowing that God will fend off
The virus for those whose faith
Equals his. His voice with the authority
Of the great puritans
Bent to send grandmothers
To the hangman or burn
A beautiful woman into
A hag of ash. He burns
With the fire of vanity,
How God will listen to his protestations.
No one loves the divinity
As he must. High or low
Churchman, he throws wide the door
And humbled, they enter
Clutching their bibles.
His sermon, this early spring Sunday,

Glorifies rebirth, how nothing,
Nothing, but God's love is needed.
The Satanic virus cannot take
The baptized who forsake dread
To praise the Lord in congress.
Here in the hard pews of the hard love of God.
The fear-not advocacy of the
Great Awakening reddens his face.
This is the passion God wants of us.
How his son defied the Pharisees
And shouldered the cross
To rise again; his voice soaring
Like the bird of prey,
The falcon angel. Come unmasked,
Clasp hands and kiss, he commands.
Weeks later, gasping, he refuses
The paramedics, the ventilator
That roisters breath into the
Stiffening lungs. If God
Seems speechless to his congregation,
Think how awestruck they will be
On the third day when his tomb opens
And he steps out girdled in the light.

Joan Colby has published widely in journals such as *Poetry, Atlanta Review, South Dakota Review, Gargoyle, Pinyon, Little Patuxent Review, Spillway, Midwestern Gothic* and others. Awards include two Illinois Arts Council Literary Awards and an Illinois Arts Council Fellowship in Literature. She has published 21 books including *Selected Poems* from FutureCycle Press which received the 2013 FutureCycle Prize and *Ribcage* from Glass Lyre Press which has been awarded the 2015 Kithara Book Prize. Three of her poems have been featured on *Verse Daily* and another is among the winners of the 2016 Atlanta Review International Poetry Contest. Her newest books are *Carnival* from FutureCycle Press, *The Seven Heavenly Virtues* from Kelsay Books and *Her Heartsongs* from Presa Press.. Colby is a senior editor of FutureCycle Press and an associate editor of *Good Works Review*. Website: www.joancolby.com. Facebook: Joan Colby. Twitter: poetjm.

Six Bells (3 A.M.)
Karla Linn Merrifield

Like a ship, this kiss will never sleep.
Even in the wee hours, it rises from my heart
to man the bridge through weather fair and foul;

slips from my tongue to command
the engine control console even now
blipping and blinking with electronic pulses;

threads the narrows between my teeth,
taking a nip with it a la galley knives
even now deftly slicing and dicing;

and it sweeps from my mouth with the panache
of a dancer even now in the emptied ballroom,
performing a samba of her imagination.

This kiss will never sleep—until it is at last
decommissioned, having come to rest on your lips.

Karla Linn Merrifield has had 800+ poems appear in dozens of journals and anthologies. She has 14 books to her credit. Following her 2018 *Psyche's Scroll* (Poetry Box Select) is the 2019 full-length *Athabaskan Fractal: Poems of the Far North* from Cirque Press. She lives in New York and is currently at work on a poetry collection, *My Body the Guitar*, inspired by famous guitarists and their guitars to be published by Before Your Quiet Eyes Hologrfaph Series (Rochester, New York) in late 2021.

Doppelganger

Gene Twaronite

As the young woman
leaned across the bar
to inform me I was
her doppelganger
I did a double take
in light of the fact
that she lacked
a silver beard
and was every
bit as ebony
as I am ivory
but what she
really meant was
her style double
since she fancied
my Akubra hat
and the way it
pulled together
my casual rock
t-shirt look
an exact replica
of the look
she hoped to
someday create
and I went home
sensing the presence
of another inside me
who looked at her
face in the mirror
and saw mine

Gene Twaronite is a Tucson poet and the author of nine books, including collections of poetry, short stories and essays as well as two juvenile fantasy novels. His latest book is *My Life as a Sperm: Essays from the Absurd Side*. Follow more of his writing @thetwaronitezone.com.

Shelter at Home
Timothy Robbins

Now Mike, along with all the
rest, has moved his class on-
line. Now Mike, at the school's
behest, must get his ass in gear
and electronically opine. Now,

bettering the best, he takes an
empty glass and turns air to
algebraic wine. I love the sound
of him lecturing in his room,
going on and on about theorem

and proof. Now on his students'
screens he's a guest. He learned
Zoom to convey the shared doom
that keeps him under our roof.
For this he feels blessed. He's

a tad agoraphobic, prefers to
stay in the house. Come, let's
press our ears to the door. How
firm he sounds on Pythagoras,
like Alexander's mentor; he

(who in restaurants is usually as
discreet as a mouse) is Stentor.
What's that he's saying? He's
starting to cuss! That we too
were theorem till he proved us?

Timothy Robbins has been teaching English as a Second Language for 28 years. His poems have appeared in *Main Street Rag, Off The Coast, Bayou Magazine, Slant, Tipton Poetry Journal, Cholla Needles* and many others. He has published three volumes of poetry: *Three New Poets* (Hanging Loose Press), *Denny's Arbor Vitae* (Adelaide Books) and *Carrying Bodies* (Main Street Rag Press). He lives in Wisconsin with his husband of 22 years.

I am afraid of Virginia Woolf
Christian Lozada

My wife and I are living *Idiocracy*
the movie about the dumbing-down of the world,
because we're too smart to have unplanned kids
unlike our families
who seem to multiply like gremlins
and have a child every time they bathe

Lessa and I are living *Who's Afraid of Virginia Woolf*
and have a child named Sherman
he's fat like me
obnoxious like her
funny and whiny at the same time
he loves to read
hates the outside world
lectures us on the food we eat
because we eat only candy and meat in front of him
while he has to enjoy his carrots

We hope to have a daughter, too
and think about calling her Alexie
but she might mean we can't revisit family
from embarrassment of our quirkiness

Christian Lozada is the product of an immigrant Filipino and Daughter of the American Revolution and has co-written the poetry book *Leave with More Than You Came With*, published by Arroyo Secco Press and a photographic history book *Hawaiians in Los Angeles*. Poetry has been anthologized in *Gutters and Alleyways: Poems on Poverty*, (Cadence Collective), and his poems and stories have appeared in *Hawaii Pacific Review* (forthcoming), *Dryland: A Literary Journal, A&U Magazine, Spot Literary Journal, Blue Collar Review* and various other journals. Christian has hosted the Read on till Morning literary series and Harbor College Poetry Night, and invited to read or speak at the Autry Museum, the Twin Towers Correctional Facility, and other places throughout Southern California.

Odes to Satan
William Doreski

Witches' sabbath comes around
again, bears at the bird feeder,
rain drooling from the eaves.

You wanted a decent silence
to roll over and flatten the land,
refreshing us with wildflowers,

which ghosts of the fallen tribes
acknowledge in their language
and value for medicinal use.

We could use some good medicine
now that the plague is churning
in cities gone gray with distance,

as Dickinson seemed to predict.
The few surviving witches
are a surly lot, their magic

abused by politicians eager
for re-election, misused
by economists bent on proving

that wealth deserves its cache.
You hope the rain clears by dark
so we can join the witches

romping around their barbecue
in the heart of the heart of forest.
I'd rather stay home and watch

TV shows from my childhood,
when everything was black and white.
I'd rather drink ginger tea and nod

with mortal sleep than listen

to gnarled figures chanting
their trite little odes to Satan,

who has done his work on earth
and left us gazing into mirrors
to study our wrinkled grins.

The day decants in weather
the color of last winter's socks.
Hyacinth and daffodils smirk.

Maybe there won't be a sabbath
celebrated in the woods behind
our house. Maybe the loggers

felled too many trees, allowing
sun and moonlight to sterilize
the mossy places of sacrifice

where night-vapors fostered dreams
innocent people like us
mistook for our daily lives.

William Doreski lives in New Hampshire. His work has appeared in various journals and in several collections, most recently *Train to Providence*, a collaboration with photographer Rodger Kingston.

Second Child
Charles Grosel

She's body where he's mind,
the way she squeals her laughter
when you swing her through the air,
squeezes applesauce through her fingers
rubs it in her hair as if this is the most
fun you can have on all fours,
until she finds the flour
and the strawberry jello
and transmutes them
with her private alchemy.
She's comfortable in her skin
in a way her brother is not,
nor we her parents,
each of us measuring joy
in tiny spoons.
She grabs it by the fist,
stuffs it in her ears,
smears it on the high chair tray
for all the world to see.

Charles Grosel is an editor, writer, and poet living in Arizona. He has published stories in *Western Humanities Review, Fiction Southeast, Red Cedar Review, Water-Stone,* and *The MacGuffin* and poems in *Slate, The Threepenny Review, Poet Lore, Cream City Review* and *Harpur Palate,* among others. *The Sound of Rain Without Water,* a chapbook of poems, is coming out in the next year.

A Moonlight Tryst
Shelby Stephenson

A closing of a door slides motes to dust
And brings a hovering close to clinging,
The space of then and now a blood-dry thirst
I try to leave alone, photos singing
Her yearning, mine, which keeps me in our lives
A singing, bending posture, heat and drive.

And when our clothes no longer stay attached
To anyone cognition spells with kind
Profusions breathing squelches at our backs,
We front the one and two the same *I am*
A love of rites allows to privacy,
While throw-rugs hold composure, irony.

On edge of bed she settles like a swan
Upheld for past's mercurial feathers,
Abiding functions making sure her brawn
From childhood means love of countless weathers
On multiplicity set to dial lots
Of clothes she prefers, especially tops.
                              I want to start

My car for home.
A long and pausing embrace stands to creep
Along the surfacing moons on the pane,
The curtains lying like small whales asleep
In shallows made for fools whiling the same
Old things away first lovers found in lieu
Of pleasure-groans in falling spring in tune.

Shelby Stephenson was North Carolina's poet laureate 2015-18 and editor of *Pembroke Magazine* for 32 years. His current book of poems: *Slavery and Freedom on Paul's Hill.*

Indiana Bildungsroman
Samantha Fain

That tulip tree looked
nothing like my mother
but it kept me alive.

Bad habits found me
faster than I could drive the tractor:

I prayed tomato stains out of shirts,
skipped all the funerals,
dreamed of how much distance
I could weave between
my fingers & my father's.

The house remained the same
shade of lemon even when
I jumped forward & backward in time

—I wouldn't read Vonnegut
til I was already gone—

& everything needled me.
I leaned on barbed wire
while I play-smoked cattails
with seedlings of sophistication.

There were homecomings,
the football & the dying—
I didn't even care.

When I left,
I shrugged off the city
like a shawl
& felt a whole new
kind of cold.

At the Indianapolis 500, They Spill Milk on Purpose
Samantha Fain

I am crying without reason, again, teapotting all over the place.
Every breath messes, leaves fusses of hair & tufts of rain.
I write poems backwards, beginning with the end,
sharing a meal with closure & entropy. We dine. We wail.
We rise, phoenixish. Rock bottom, too, melts eventually.
Yet the corn invariably gets planted. Only scientists can break glass
& justify chaos. Think about life without our water.
Our bodies would be so dry. The good thing about boom & bust cycles
are the booms, which are almost always next: bursts of beauty
everywhere, like how moss can grow on just about anything.

Samantha Fain is an MFA candidate at Bowling Green State University. She studied creative writing at Franklin College. Her work has appeared in The *Indianapolis Review, SWWIM, Utterance,* and others. She tweets at @samcanliftacar.

First Pitch 2020
Richard Krohn

He never makes it to the mound, halting at home
to assault the mic as film crews kneel before him.
Big as The Babe after all those franks, blonded
strands flapping from his cap as the delayed voice,

a great un-Gehrig, echoes off empty seats, *a record
crowd,* he'll claim, *after so many canceled games,
which would've been more if I hadn't seen before
the experts, how nasty this virus was, but now*

*to show how America's Been Made Great Again,
my idea to set the 4th aside as never before,
if you're a student of history like I was, and headed
for the majors, some said, knocking balls over walls,*

*I mean, it's 1 against 9, or 13 if you count the umps,
who oughta be ashamed, 4 Blind Mice, I call them,*
mock-stumbling from the box, arms outstretched,
eyes closed, then feeling his way back at the mic

to cup a hand behind his ear, as if waiting for his rally
to swell into *Boo!* saying now how he played short
*like a la-*teen-*O,* the O reverbing beyond the bleachers,
and that's what we want, immigrants with talent,

*not rapists and drug-dealing gangs, dudes as bad
as this virus from China! which I alone stopped,
though the dishonest media didn't give me credit,
human scum, most of them, and corrupt, like sign-*

*stealing Obama, and Hilary, crooked as a knuckle
curve and slimy as a spitter, but I beat her bad,
like an old rug, the virus, too, in record time,
so no more masks except to squat behind the plate,*

where you catch things, my instincts tell me,
and they're usually right because I've got a big one,
pointing to his cap, *but this isn't about me,*
it's about the U-S-A, so let's PLAY BALL!!

Richard Krohn lived much of his life up and down the East Coast, north and south, but with several years at various times in the Midwest and also in Central America. He presently teaches Economics and Spanish at Moravian College in Bethlehem, Pennsylvania. In recent years his poetry has appeared in *Poet Lore, Southern Poetry Review, Arts & Letters, Tar River,* and *Rattle,* among many others.

On Me(n)

Mihika Jain

Remembrance is deadly
or sweet, depending on who you ask. Ask me,
but it's your choice really, because he never did
and giving you a choice makes me a better person. Better
or meeker or weaker, depending on who you ask.
Sticking your hand in someone's vagina now there's no ambiguity there,
at least. Blue is a way of life but
he was wearing blue too-shirt, chequered, saccharine as the
hopscotch butterscotch I dropped on it. 'I'm more of a chocolate
guy' he laughed it off and the sky was lavender fire then
and the flavour of the day was giddiness.
we walked home to the lavender curtains and whitewashed walls
hand-me-downs from another country, another time
remembrance is relative and I know colours have no allegiances but
who's asking? He does
perched on the threshold his feet
bathed in suede promises.

Mihika Jain lives in India. She is a passionate writer and poet who has had her work published on various platforms. Her other interests include music, art, and politics.

Bark

David Flynn

The quarantine has been extended by the mayor, by the governor.
Indoor people.
But I want to drive, drive for hours on the interstate,
listening to music,
letting my mind wander.
Maybe a day trip back to my home town,
visiting my family graves in Calvary Cemetery.
Maybe a day trip to . . .
Anywhere.
Locked in.
But there's a pandemic outside the condo door.
Little balls with knobs attached,
according to the drawing on TV.
Little blue balls with red knobs usually.
Too small to see, but what isn't?
Nanoparticles, dark matter, microbes that inhabit our guts.
These viri apparently are selfish,
only out for their own good,
cutting off the breaths of their hosts.
I wear a mask now when I go to the store,
a black one.

And what word do I think of today, randomness to correct the correctness
of my situation?
Bark.
The rough skin of a tree.
One way we write how a dog sounds.
Of course, a tree doesn't think, I have such beautiful bark.
And a dog doesn't actually go "Bark."
If a dog were to trot up to you and say, "Bark,"
Run.
The dog also doesn't say "Woof woof."
A cat doesn't say, "Meow".
In Japan dogs supposedly said, "Won won."
We are so inexact.

Barking up the wrong tree.
Huh?
A dog climbing a tree trunk?
Why?
Why is it the wrong tree?
The squirrel is in the other tree?
Question marks too many.

Be safe.
That's what I tell everybody during this viral hibernation,
emails, phone calls, Zoom.
Be safe.
All that means is,
don't take stupid chances.
We can't actually be safe.
That stroke might happen today.
That tree might fall on my bed tonight.
That teenager might swerve into my lane tomorrow.
But try.
Be safe.
Sanitize.
Your kitchen counter.
But don't sanitize your love.
We must, after all, feel.
We die, but we will die anyway.
Feel.
Care.
Be safe.

David Flynn was born in the textile mill company town of Bemis, Tennessee. His jobs have included newspaper reporter, magazine editor and university teacher. He has five degrees and is both a Fulbright Senior Scholar and a Fulbright Senior Specialist with a recent grant in Indonesia. His literary publications total more than 220. Among the eight writing residencies he has been awarded are five at the Wurlitzer Foundation in Taos, New Mexico, and stays in Ireland and Israel. He spent a year in Japan as a member of the Japan Exchange and Teaching program. He currently lives in Nashville, Tennessee.

With Wattles Dangling Like Earrings at a Jewelry Party
Rodney Torreson

hens plump up in nesting boxes. Oval
holes hint to dim brains the shape to think on
through ovary and oviduct. Regal eggs
worked out in straw surely transcend them,
which I know nothing about at age 5,
while I learn to gather eggs in a pail and lug it
to the utility room near the kitchen.

Before the coop I loiter—my throbbing
heartbeat hobbling my hand, which I study,
like I'll not see those knuckles again.
Since the hand looks a bit like a chicken foot,
can it possibly fit in, fool the hens
when my small tender palm curves
like a shell to invade the down under?

"What you must do," my father says,
you must do alone!" So, in the sanctity of
the white chickens, my hand hesitates.
When I reach in, the squawker follows
my hand with her beak. Suddenly wings erupt
in a brush-up of my face. I'm the follower
now, watching the tenor of a feather

drifting to the floor. I try again.
She strikes my hand, pecks and pecks.
Soundly thumped, I run, fingers buzzing,
to the house—tears blubbering down
my chin. My father turns me around
to face the door: "You must reach in
as if the eggs were yours!"

I dawdle toward the chicken shed
but there, reach boldly under.
Seamlessly an egg molds to my palm.
Soon I fill a basket, each egg now bright
as if it has a pilot light. As I walk
toward the house, the egg of my head
beams as if I'm my own sun.

The poet laureate of Grand Rapids, Michigan from 2007-2010, **Rodney Torreson's** third full-length collection of poetry, *The Jukebox Was the Jury of Their Love,* was issued by Finishing Line Press in 2019. In addition, Torreson has new poems forthcoming in *American Journal of Poetry, Connecticut River Review, Main Street Rag, North Dakota Quarterly,* and *Streetlight.*

Manic Regressive
Gilbert Allen

February 28, 2017

Yes, our planet's always been
bipolar, its head
beclouded, incessantly spinning, but this
is beyond bleak or balmy—
blizzards devoured by days
in the eighties, with tornados
and droughts for dessert.

Still, the waters are rising,
glaciers waving goodbye,
islands disappearing like necklaces
during Mardi Gras, and we're all
beating our bare breasts, falling down
drunk on ignorance or knowledge,
waiting for Ash Wednesday.

Gilbert Allen's most recent collection of poems is *Catma,* from Measure Press. His book of linked stories, *The Final Days of Great American Shopping,* was published by University of South Carolina Press in 2016. A frequent contributor to TPJ, he is a member of the South Carolina Academy of Authors and the Bennette E. Geer Professor of Literature Emeritus at Furman University.

Saint Alban's
Sheila Wellehan

There's a beautiful church in my neighborhood –
its cedar shingles have aged to dark brown.
Above the entrance,
white-painted wood planks form a crucifix.
Banks of stained-glass windows
are the simple building's glory,
vivid squares of red, yellow, and blue.

I imagined redemption
as sun streamed through those windows
and prismatic patches danced on the floor.
Instead of attempting to inspire awe or reverence,
this church just said, *Welcome, we're happy you're here.*
Still, something stopped me each Sunday morning.
I stood outside. Something always held me back.

For heaven's sake, you're an agnostic,
I said to myself as I strolled by one Friday evening.
Cars had flooded the parking lot
for the weekly Alcoholics Anonymous meeting.
They lined the street blocks away.
The A.A. meetings intrigued me as much as the masses did –
I hadn't been to a meeting in too long a time.

A.A. was down in the basement, not in the chapel,
but at least I'd found a way to get through the door.
I thought traffic would diminish
with the arrival of lovely spring weather,
but as temperatures rose, the crowds just grew –
it's been a year since I found out about that meeting
and I'm still watching from the outside.

There's a beautiful church in my neighborhood.
The design beams and the people entering smile.
I walk right by when I'm out wandering.
I can't go in.
I'm afraid of what's inside.

Sheila Wellehan's poetry is featured in *Menacing Hedge, Rust + Moth, Thimble Literary Magazine, Tinderbox Poetry Journal, Whale Road Review*, and many other journals and anthologies. She lives in Cape Elizabeth, Maine. Visit her online at www.sheilawellehan.com.

Visiting My Autistic Sister
David M. Alper

Like a stream, she resides between
the shiver and the skin
that grasps her shadow.

This is where retention commences:
the thread of what must be lifts
from the braid of what was

and hinges inside her now, her present.
My sister sways, gone, or gone again
and totters like a blade of grass swept

by an odd April wind, no more tethered
to the past than to the bed on which she sits.
She runs her palm against the side of my head:

a new shadow falls, a shiver stirs off the wall,
and her wind quenches the flame of life's lantern
with us dancing to see her new dawn.

David M. Alper is a high school AP English teacher in New York City, residing in Manhattan. His work has appeared in *Thirty West Publishing House, OPEN: Journal of Arts & Letters, Glassworks Magazine*, and elsewhere.

Spinning the Pandemic's Stay Home Order
Janet Reed

My neighbor says he found wildflower seeds at Dollar General, this basket of pansies at Wal-Mart. No quarantine is going to deny him his spring. "It's just a cold," he tells me. "America's lost its damned mind."

To the purple petals basketed on a shepherd's hook, he adds a flag, a stripe of red starred blue
stapled to a stick made for such display.

We stare at each other across a bed of hostas in our shared courtyard just beginning to unfurl their green swag in a world much changed from the one they left in December's hard freeze. "New York," I offer.
Only a week or two into this sick, New York numbers on cable news keep me home. "We don't want to be New York."

The way his eyes slip behind their lids, lips thin, he must thought I said "zombies crossed the Brooklyn Bridge."

"It's just the flu."

In the bed of hostas, he's staked a pinwheel, a plastic bike decked out in the colors of freedom, its red, white, and blue wheels manic in the wind, as if throttle open, it might leap the sidewalk and forsythias that separate us, make its mark in some daredevil stunt.

He's running all over seeking roots in seeds, baskets, plastics.

Once, I, too, crowded my porch with pots of petals glorious for a day or two. I tended and pruned past their season and emptied the leggy remnants into September's dumpster. I want to tell him that pansies only last a season and only if aphids leave them be, if blackberry winter doesn't linger, if spring rains don't deluge. So many ifs that in this season sound like if we wash our hands, if we wear a mask, if we stay home.

These days I want to be the hostas. Less flash, more symmetry. Roots knotted in the earth tight as cables suspending the deck of the unknown, strong enough to hold their place in this world.

The neighbor keeps planting flags and flowers while the wheels of the bike churn to leave the ground. I expect I'll find their stars scattered, stripes shredded in our shared yard by morning, a cargo of broken bones, collateral damage, while the hostas brunt the sun on their leaf backs.

Quarantine Slow
Janet Reed

Mrs. Dallaway said she would buy the flowers herself. Virginia Woolf

Today the rain gauzes the ground, hiding
the plague that keeps me inside, the walls
in this apartment musk heavy with weeks
of greasy quarantine. Even the dog
stumbles slow to lick her bowl.
We are bears furred thick in drugged sleep.

Death crawls around us. The man
in the unit below left yesterday zipped
in a body bag, a wellness check unwell,
despite the *stay away* note taped
to his door when this sick began:
because of the virus, he'd said.

Outside, the cherry tree's white flowers
hang limp as tissues wadded in tears.
One leafless limb stands sentinel
in its center, a scar in this kingdom
of promise, the bareness of rigor
mortis an eel-sized wound on a fleshy

landscape. In the days before the rain,
that tree was a symphony of sepals,
pink-throats singing *gloria in excelsis deo*.
Likewise, the redbuds and azaleas rocked
the gospel blues in revival shades of purple
brilliant enough to make the devil shout

for Jesus. Forgive me my withering.
Tomorrow, I will buy a Dahlia for my porch,
yellow as sun, petals big as dinner plates,
plant it in a pot I can water & feed until its roots
bind boundaries I will then prune and pot again.
Let me pretend I can remake this world.

Janet Reed earned a Master's degree in English Literature from Pittsburg State University in Kansas. She currently teaches writing and literature at Crowder College in Missouri. She has work published in multiple journals with more forthcoming.

Transplanted
D.C. Buschmann

Blistering rays
off Nature's mirror
withered
my would-be blooms
still in the bud.

Nurturing mentors
found healthy soil
and proper moisture
and just the right sunlight
for me to relocate,
to thrive
        unhampered

My new home
required constant
composting
to keep my roots
        fertile and free.

My limbs grew wide
and tall. Avid gardeners
pruned me. In time,
others picked fruit
off many branches
        cultivated unencumbered.

[This poem was first published in *Red Coyote*]

D.C. Buschmann is a retired editor and reading specialist. Her poem, "Death Comes for a Friend," was the Editor's Choice in *Poetry Quarterly*, Winter 2018. She has been published in the US, the UK, Australia, Iraq, and India, including Kurt Vonnegut Museum and Library's *So it Goes Literary Journal, Flying Island, The Adirondack Review, San Pedro River Review, Better Than Starbucks, Rat's Ass Review, Nerve Cowboy,* and elsewhere. She lives in Carmel, Indiana with husband Nick and miniature schnauzers Cupcake and Coco. Her first full collection of poetry will be published in 2020.

Plaster Saint
Laura Saint Martin

My nosy neighbor pauses to peruse
my overgrown garden that allegedly
prevents passage through the community walkway;
poses to elicit a few nuisance barks
from my nuisance dog.
She is a beautiful woman, in her bogus beatitude,
armored eyes preempting light where
bile bivouacs.
Her tectonic jaws gnaw at petty resentments, thirty two
pearly white axes to grind.
I imagine her awake at night, next to her limp husband,
her caged coiffure grown as unruly as my lavender,
my passion vine twining itself
where air should go.

Laura Saint Martin is a writer of fiction and poetry, with several short pieces published in online journals and print anthologies. She lives in Rancho Cucamonga, California.

Graveyard Gnosis
Daniel E. Blackston

Your breath will end without you.
Your skin will wither without you.
Your eyes will go blind without you.
Your heart will collapse without you.
Your blood will be dust without you.
Your brain will shrivel without you.
Your hands will feed worms without you.
Your lips will turn to mud without you.
Your spine will dissolve without you.
Your bones will be clay without you.
Your spirit will go on.
With or without you.

Daniel Blackston is a professional writer and musician who lives and works in Springfield, Illinois.

An Exhibition
Anne Whitehouse

An exhibition is not
the conclusion to a project,
but the opening to a conversation.
It is the context that matters
as much as the objects themselves,
connections made for the first time
or revived from the well of forgetfulness.

How to design a curve
using only straight lines
so even a novice can build it.

Anne Whitehouse is the author of six poetry collections, most recently *Meteor Shower* (Dos Madres Press, 2016). She has also written a novel, *Fall Love*, which is now available in Spanish translation as *Amigos y amantes* by Compton Press. Recent honors include 2018 Prize Americana for Prose, 2017 Adelaide Literary Award in Fiction, 2016 Songs of Eretz Poetry Prize, 2016 Common Good Books' Poems of Gratitude Contest, 2016 RhymeOn! Poetry Prize, 2016 F. Scott and Zelda Fitzgerald Museum Poetry Prize. She lives in New York City.

www.annewhitehouse.com

Lullwater Park Odyssey (Beside the Children's Hospital)
Kelly Whiddon

The city is warm with car engines
and hot rain. For weeks, you've walked
this found park where the trees
go on and back in ceaseless rows
forever, a hammerspace, nature's
clown car.

It's a walking park. You step into
a long quiet until you pass through
something like time and stumble
on a span bridge to a 1920's
power-house, a waterfall,
a Tudor-style mansion.
You see others, runners,

or people like you,
dazed and wandering. You
have eaten buffalo meat
and wild petals. You have cried
into the lake, watched fish
and waterfowl.

You are here to escape
the hospital where you're asked
if you want to hold your child
for the first time, if you want
him off the machines.

He's not dead yet.
He will be soon. The notion
seems barbaric, but the disorganized
mind wants to hold the child.

There's a lovely blindness
to life. With death you open a door
and the knob falls off
in your hand; you climb
a stair and find the last step
missing. You fall
and fall.

But here, when you walk,
there is always more to see.
It's a lotus-eating park, you think.
One day, you'll tumble out
and find you've aged
a thousand years.

Kelly Whiddon lives in Georgia and has published in *Crab Orchard Review, Southeast Review, Poetry International, Southern Poetry Review,* and *Meridian,* among others. Her book, *The House Began to Pitch* (Mercer UP), was honored with the Adrienne Bond Poetry Award, and she has served as associate editor of *Apalachee Review* and is on the staff of *International Quarterly.* You can find more info at www.kellywhiddon.com.

The Corn Block
Lorne Mook

The trail where I go to walk alone
has changed now that it's August. (I had forgotten
to expect it to happen.) The corn is higher than
head high and thickened as if someone
who opened the Book of the Land and with a crayon
scored lines across an empty shape had gone
back to the shape and filled it completely in.
The corn, exhaling its hot oxygen,
blocking the wind, could be the incarnation
of all those spirits, previously unseen,
who wall the winds that sometimes blow between
you and you and you and the me within.

Lorne Mook grew up on a farm in northwest Pennsylvania and now lives in Upland, Indiana, where he is Associate Professor of English at Taylor University. In 2011 he published the first English translation of Rainer Maria Rilke's third book of poems, *Dream-Crowned*. His translations have also appeared *in AGNI, Poetry International, Literary Imagination*, and other journals. A collection of his own poems, *Travelers Without Maps*, was published in 2002.

The Animals
Maree Reedman

There are no guns in heaven
so all the animals he'd abused
followed him like he was the Pied Piper,
asking, *Why?*
His mother's tabby Tiger
he kicked down the stairs,
the curlews set on fire, the tom
drowned in his garbage bin for pissing
on his BBQ. The kangaroos and emus
run down in his Polaris,
the ducks he shot into pink oblivion.

The headless ducks trailed him, being forgiving
creatures, mistaking his twitching fingers
for breaking bread. The curlews kept clear
but that's how they behaved with everyone.
The cats were less charitable, clawed
his ankles at night when he watched TV.
The emus headbutted him whenever they had the chance
and the roos kickboxed his coward's belly.
Still, his fingers twitched for the trigger:
all these animals to kill and no means to do it.

Most people improved when confronted with their sins
but after a few weeks, the animals agreed
he hadn't made any progress.
They called a special meeting with the shaman,
who looked into the man's soul. He saw a starving
child who had eaten most of his own heart.
It was time to summon the mother.
She spent time with the shaman and knew what to do.

The man bawled when he saw her,
the animals dumbfounded,
they did not think him capable of love.
The man clung to his mother
for many nights, as if he was a baby
who needed suckling.

They spent eternity together,
sat by the lake and fed the ducks grapes,
laughing at the ganders honking and flapping
their wings, reminding them of his old ways,
Tiger curled on his lap.

Maree Reedman lives in Brisbane, Australia with one husband, two cockatiels, and five ukuleles. Her poetry has appeared or is forthcoming in Australia and the United States in *The Chiron Review, StylusLit, Unbroken, Hecate*, and other places. Her poetry has won awards in The Ipswich Poetry Feast. She loves poetry that tells a good story.

A Theft of Crutches Leaves Everyone Lame
Denise Thompson-Slaughter

Mark Twain's greatest regret
was that he'd convinced his wife
there was no afterlife.

Later, when she lay dying in grievous pain,
he could see what he'd done:
robbed her of hope and comfort
in her last days.

That deathbed stare: despair!
The only unforgiveable sin, supposedly,
is that against the Holy Ghost.

Neither, Twain found, could he forgive himself.

Mourning Tote
Denise Thompson-Slaughter

Mourning comes, the darkness stays.
We think of all the thousand ways
we're fragile and prone to mistake,
while others we for granted take.

We counted on those who cut our hair,
who made us smile, who loved to share,
who treated our pets and our maladies
in better times, by far, than these.

We dream of those whom we have lost
and watch the rose poke through the frost.
The year advances as it will,
but we tote up our losses still.

Denise Thompson-Slaughter is a writer living in Western New York. Her published work includes two books of poetry (*Sixty-ish: Full Circle,* Spirited Muse Press, 2017; and *Elemental,* Plain View Press, 2010), a novella (*Mystery Gifts,* Spirited Muse Press, 2018), a couple of short stories, and a handful of brief memoir pieces, the most recent of which was published in the May issue of *Dash Literary Journal.*

Doris as a Third Grader

R. Nikolas Macioci

"Come sit with me," her father says. "We'll go
over your times tables." She rises from
the living room floor where she has been cutting
paper dolls, pulls a stool next to her dad.
"I'll say the problem, and you give the answer."
He is patient as God and more important
to her than any of her dolls. "You're very
good with numbers," he tells her. She smiles.

Her mother appears in the doorway howling
about Doris not cleaning her room, needing
to get ready for bed, and that he is spoiling her
with too much attention.

Her father tells her to put away
the multiplication chart and prepare
for bed. "You're too soft with her,"
the mother screeches.

Doris climbs steps to the bathroom, brushes
her teeth, stands looking in the mirror,
feels an aversion to her own reflection.
She turns off the light, slumps to her bed,
gets in, and hugs her Disney princess doll.

Outside, snow blows past the window
and under the security light like
a stream of unwanted white ants.

R. Nikolas Macioci earned a PhD from The Ohio State University. OCTELA, the Ohio Council of Teachers of English, named Nik Macioci the best secondary English teacher in the state of Ohio. Nik is the author of two chapbooks as well as six books: More than two hundred of his poems have been published here and abroad, including *The Society of Classic Poets Journal, Chiron, The Comstock Review, Concho River Review,* and *Blue Unicorn.* Forthcoming books are *Rough* and *Why Dance?*

Words Count
Bruce Levine

Words count
A harbinger of fate
No more
No less
Than primordial rites
Following tangents
Toward fulfillment
Along an existential course
Resolved
In reflex motion
Predicated on words

Bruce Levine, a 2019 Pushcart Prize Poetry Nominee, has spent his life as a writer of fiction and poetry and as a music and theatre professional. Over 300 of his works are published in over 25 on-line journals including *Ariel Chart, Friday Flash Fiction, Literary Yard;* over 30 print books including *Poetry Quarterly, Haiku Journal, Dual Coast Magazine,* and his shows have been produced in New York and around the country. Six eBooks are available from Amazon.com. His work is dedicated to the loving memory of his late wife, Lydia Franklin. He lives in New York with his dog, Daisy. Visit him at www.brucelevine.com.

One Septillion Stars
Michael Estabrook

At one time
I was very interested
in Astronomy
knew about the planets
and their moons
types and distances of stars
and galaxies, about comets
meteors, asteroids
black holes and supernovae.

The universe includes all matter found in galaxies and in intergalactic space: atomic particles followed by atoms, molecules, dust, space rocks, comets, asteroids, moons, dwarf planets, planets, solar systems, stars, black holes, nebulae, galaxies, dark energy and dark matter. (According to BioEd Online).

At one time
I could lie on my back
on a grassy hill
at night
point out Ursa the Bear
Orion the Hunter, Taurus
the Bull and all
the rest of the pantheon.

The Sun is just one of over 100 billion stars in our Milky Way Galaxy, and the Milky Way is just one of over 100 billion galaxies in the known universe which equals: 1,000,000,000,000,000,000,000,000 or a "1" with 24 zeros after it – one septillion stars. Only a rough number, however.

But now I never
can get to it. Life
has snagged me by the toe
so many other things to do
so many other things
in the way.

But I miss it. I really do miss it.

Michael Estabrook has been publishing his poetry in the small press since the 1980s. He has published over 20 collections, a recent one being *The Poet's Curse, A Miscellany* (The Poetry Box, 2019). He lives in Massachusetts.

The Morning After
Jennifer McClellan

Today
I might do it.

My nerve is high enough to touch
the sky full of hopeful clouds.
My fingers grip the wheel,
with chipped purple polish.
Mr Brightside vibrates the air,
and I might keep driving past the building
where people expect me to show up.

The highway calls my name.
Her possibilities spin beneath me; she knows
I want to press my hands into a fresh pile of clay,
be inspired by a more creative place!
I want...I want. Is it possible
to know what I actually want?
I swear I might keep driving to find out.
But then

the early sunlight meets my ring
like your hand on the back of my knee.
when we burned in the August air,
barely breathing through my curtain of hair.
Last night was therapy; your arms
around me, healed me
as we stayed up too late.
Last night was encouragement.
Damn it, we're going to do something, some day!
Last night's conversation reminded me
that we've already built a love we'd both die for,
and that's a hell of a creation.

I sigh as the song ends,
and my nerve fades.
I signal and turn left into the lot.
I park my car, walk to the building,
and clock in.

Jennifer McClellan is an Evansville, Indiana poet based poet. She has written poetry since she was a teenager, though this is her first time appearing in a literary journal. She believes poetry and music are the heart of human connection and is thrilled to share her writing.

Elegy for a Traveling Consultant

Brooke Dwojak Lehmann

That year I worked in Philadelphia,
and I cried each time I packed my suitcase.

On the Mondays that ended early,
I strolled through Macy's

sashaying through glittery shoes,
on ivory marble floors,

the Wanamaker Organ jolting
me from a phantom reel.

The evening recital became my respite
from a life that felt borrowed –

Walnut Street, Palomar Hotel,
mandatory *happy hours,*

snow falling in late March,
alone in my bedsheets.

Most days, I walked to the office,
except when rain showers soaked

the black and gold leather Tory flats
that a decade later, rest in my closet.

When summer arrived,
I ran through the city at night

like a breathless fugitive
down by the humid river

that made it feel hotter
than the South

where I longed to be back home.

Brooke Dwojak Lehmann holds a B.S.in Chemical Engineering from Purdue University. Poetry has been published by *Black Fox Literary Magazine* and *Parentheses*. Brooke lives in Seattle where she freelances as a fashion model and consultant.

You Can Neither Urge Nor Resist
Kit Kennedy

Encircling you
a thimble of green

may be hidden
beyond the echo

of what you thought
you could see, could touch

Watch deeply
listen

to these trees
wrap yourself in their texture

learn to paint their bark
into your dreams

Kit Kennedy is a queer elder living in Walnut Creek, California. She has published 7 collections including "while eating oysters" (CLWN WR BKS, Brooklyn, NY). Work has appeared in *Tipton Poetry Journal, Great Weather for Media, First Literary Review-East, Gyroscope, Glass,* among others. She serves as Poet in Residence of SF Bay Times and Resident Poet at Ebenezer Lutheran "herchurch." Please visit: http://poetrybites.blogspot.com

Evanescence
Tim Hawkins

In the midst of a gathering blizzard of mayflies,
individuals begin to materialize
from out of the furious, coupling mass
intent on a singular purpose—to mate
with the Pale Morning Dun at the end of my line;
and I find that I pity this mildly, ironic fate—

these ephemeral creatures wasting the one shot in their lives
at procreation, (instinct, desire...love? call it what you will)
on a knotted tangle of deer hair and twine.

Though often generalized into fantasy, fetish, or love divine
aren't all such "loves" and the others found on heaven and earth,
agape and those we learned in Sunday School
including the benevolent smile of the sainted fool,

aimed at the particular, the individual,
(including our regard for our lonely selves,
and even the sanctified love of a parent for her child)
and our estimation of his, and her, and our own worth?

How can anyone say he loves humankind?
Why would Christ want to save that teeming congregation?

Witness the mayfly, and one can't help but think
of the bison, the wildebeest, and the bee,
the shimmering masses in the sea,
and the scurrying multitudes of every nation.

We all want so badly to endure,
to wake into permanence from out of our dream,
when, really, we should be treasured and adored
like the glorious mayfly, for our evanescence,

a certain glance of sunlight on the stream
in a cathedral of moss, and heron, and pine.

Tim Hawkins' short fiction and poetry can be found in many print and online magazines and anthologies. He has published a poetry collection, *Wanderings at Deadline* (Aldrich Press, 2012), a poetry chapbook, *Jeremiad Johnson* (In Case of Emergency Press, 2019), and a story and poetry chapbook, *Synchronized Swimmers* (KYSO Flash Press, 2019). His second full-length poetry collection, *West of the Backstory*, is forthcoming in late 2020 from Fernwood Press. Tim lives in Michigan. Find out more at his website: www.timhawkinspoetry.com

For Wang Wei, A Poem
Ryan David Leack

These twelve-hundred years passed
since you roamed shoreline depths,
how many generations,
generations,

warmed by the same
cloud-swept sun,
cooled by the same low moon
and its star-far desperation.

Little has changed in all that time.
I, too, wake to the sound
of passing carts,
waiting for something—

dogwood dreams
beyond city walls,
a desire to be
empty,
emptied.

Yet there are fewer bird calls.
Sometimes a finch
sings alone,
barely able to rattle
the oak with his song.

Sometimes the
wind helps him along.

Du Fu said all life is
going and returning.
I wonder if it's true.
I wonder if some things leave
and never come back to you—
your black hair, ghost of itself
in twilight years,
growing whiter still,

bramble gate closed among
a lone kingfisher's trill.
I wonder how the surface
where I read reflects the light,
how I too might be
of no mind
mirroring empty sky,
lone witness
to the sound of yellow
leaves falling,

carried through air to
open graves on ground,
frail spirits small—
untethered, unbound.

As night rises,
dust settles.
Idleness.
Somewhere East,
bamboo rustles,
falls back into place—

empty mind
empty dark

on the verge
of vanishing

I close my iron gate,
inhabit my absence,
knowing empty,
sounds of moths dancing
in false light.

Dr. Ryan David Leack teaches writing and rhetoric at the University of Southern California. He's published poetry in *Chiron Review, Pif, and Westwind*, among other journals, and also served as Editor-in-Chief of *Pomona Valley Review* for seven years.

The Doctor and The Crow
David Spicer

I met the doctor at one of my tapestry shows.
In a charcoal pantsuit and burgundy scarf,
she said, *I love your work with its shadows*

and castles, moors and horns, its blue suns,
its sienna moons. I'd like to commission
a cloth painting. She asked me to drive

eighty miles into country woods
scattered with willows, gravel crunching
under the truck tires. I arrived at a two-story

near a lake she named Memory, pancakes
cooking in the kitchen, saw *Animal Planet*
on a flat screen. We sipped small talk and coffee

until I asked, *What do you want me to make?*
She called at the stairs, *Sheryl, come here.*
I heard the shutters flutter, then *Caw, Caw,*

as a cloud-colored crow flew in a curve to us
and landed on the doctor's palm. The crow
tilted her head, pierced my eyes with hers,

nodded at the doctor. I accepted the job,
saying, *Why'd you name her Sheryl?*
She said. *I didn't. When she came to me,*

wings broken, legs damaged, she told me her name.
I can't fault her wit. I sketched Sheryl, who stared,
cawed while we discussed birds, healing, art.

Weeks later, I returned in my van,
the large artwork covered in burlap.
Groaning, we lugged it to the den,

unveiled its silk, crepe, satin, and chenille glory,
the linen bird in the center, her turquoise eyes
peering beyond ours at another world's wind

we couldn't see. *Sheryl, here,* the doctor said,
and the bird swooped down to the picture, peered at it,
jutting her head sideways, up and down, flew upstairs

without a *Caw. Hmm,* the doctor said, *I think
she likes it.* We said goodbye, but she phoned
weeks later. *How are you and Sheryl?* I asked.

The doctor said, *Fine. Or we were. She kept
looking at the picture, then her eyes told me,
'The healing's done. I may visit our friend.'*

I said, *I wonder what's on her mind.*
Maybe to do what crows do, she said.
I'm waiting for Sheryl and finishing

her portrait, her wings and body flying
downstairs to me and my shoulder,
waving a burgundy scarf with her beak.

David Spicer lives in Memphis and has published poems in *The American Poetry Review, CircleStreet, Gargoyle, Moria, Oyster River Pages, Ploughshares, Remington Review, Santa Clara Review, The Sheepshead Review, Steam Ticket, Synaeresis, Third Wednesday*, and elsewhere. Nominated for a Best of the Net three times and a Pushcart twice, he is author of six chapbooks, the latest being *Tribe of Two* (Seven CirclePress). His latest full-length collections, *American Maniac* (Hekate Publishing) and *Confessional* (Cyberwit.net), are now available. His website is www.davidspicer76.com.

Darkness Unspooling
Doris Lynch

Blackness rises from earth
toward sky. The sky laps
each rose-infused sunset; its peach rays,
and strawberry liqueurs meld clouds.

Into the gloaming, a woman
walks backwards, a woman
wearing a facemask who trusts
she will not stumble into a pothole,
ankle-whack a curb, or graze a slow-going
possum. Each night a woman walks
backward deeper into the twilight of her life.

Darkness allows possibility,
cloaks the unknown, stills the wanting
tree inside us. Darkness's penumbra
ponders past seeing.

Even over the city, the stars
watch, wait, share their small
cascades of corona light.
They reveal and hide,
travel across the universe
toward us sheltered
in daylight and darkness.

A meteorite wakens us to
the possibility of dawn—the way
three Puebloans chanted to the sun
one morning in the meadow
by my tent in Chaco Canyon.
Under fading stars,
thousand-year old songs
call up our one bright Sol
with its heat and light.

Doris Lynch lives in Bloomington, Indiana and has recent work in *Flying Island, Frogpond, Modern Haiku, Contemporary Haibun Online, Drifting Sands Haibun* and in the anthologies: *Cowboys & Cocktails: Poetry from the True Grit Saloon* (Brick Street Poetry Inc., 2019), *Red River book of Haibun* (Red River Press, New Delhi, India, 2019), and *Another Trip Around the Sun: 365 Days of Haiku for Children Young and Old,* (Brooks Books, 2019).

How long will it last?
M. Ait Ali

Somewhere here,
where the Russians
commit more crimes
against bottled & unbottled vodka.—

Where the blue-lipped French
rejoice in the news of
the arrival of a new revolution
against themselves,—looking
to be free from getting things right
for too long, for half-thought aeons.—

Where the Italians are
half tigers, half Michelangelos,
sculpting hefty, sinful lines
in time and wind...while they murmur
to each other,
"Methinks I'm becoming a god!"

Where the Africans wound up
cogitating more than they used
to chant,—feeling every road stop sign,—
starving and thirsting underneath
the fiery sunbeams just to keep a creature
like this W*hite-man* in a god-sent palace.—
'nd when they are in the arms of Morpheus,
they dream, they dream long, and sleep-talk
aloud, saying things like,
"Hey, White-man, would you starve for me too?"

There's this young, beautiful, scarlet lady,
whose words are the last famous ones you're going to hear,—
words of utmost delight and surprise,
*"I ring no bells, I send no letters, I ring no phones,
I don't knock on doors, I don't come through windows,
I don't slide down chimneys, and here, I came, now,
to claim your soul in the midst of your excellence and comfort."*

M. Ait Ali is 28 years old, living in Agadir, Morocco and has works published in *Silly Linguistics, Nebula Adnauseum Magazine, Alien Buddha Press, Rogue Wolf Press, Spillwords,* and *A dove for peace* anthology.

Sniper
Ann Boaden

You have only a few minutes.
As you mow the lawn
or pump the gas
or load the rented rug cleaner
into the van,
you're thinking, maybe,
of the class you taught
or will teach,
of the weight of love and indifference
in that room where stray wasps dangle
against the high fluorescent sun,
or you're remembering
the sale you made
or didn't make,
or seeing again
your child's eyes in the morning,
or you're counting the errands yet to do:
the cleaners, where you'll leave a suit;
the library, where you'll pay a fine;
the supermarket
where you'll buy organic broccoli
and chicken
or ground beef under plastic,
toilet paper and Kleenex
and tartar-control toothpaste.
Or you're thinking about sex
with someone you've seen only once
or forever
or a cold beer
or a sick dog
or the raccoons making flip-top lids
of the turf in your backyard.

Or
if you're lucky
(for now you have only one minute more)
you're noticing
the maple on the hill
and
from some mysterious place in you
saying thank you thank you thank you
before you spin into darkness.

Ann Boaden is an Illinois native. After earning her master's and doctoral degrees in English from The University of Chicago, she returned to teach at her undergraduate college, Augustana (Illinois). Work has appeared in *South Dakota Review, Big Muddy, Christmas on the Great Plains* (University of Iowa Press), *The Penwood Review, ACM (Another Chicago Magazine), Sediments, The Windhover,* and *Ginosko,* among other publications.

I'm Sure You're Right, Lord
Tom C. Hunley

Lord, I hear my daughter
call *Dad* in her sleep.
I open her door. She looks at me,
or at a dream of me, then drifts back to sleep.
Now I'm in her dream as if a dream
is an FM radio and I'm a song
framed on either side by white noise.
Her hebetudinous boyfriend struts
across her dream like the star
of a 'B' horror movie in which teens
die cheesy, avoidable deaths.
My heart balls up into a fist
that can only punch my rib cage.
I want to fling my body at him
like a brick but this is her dream.
Don't wake my dad, she tells him,
and in the mirror on her dresser
I disappear before my own eyes.
Lord, I'm sure You're right
not to let me beat him up
in her dream. She'd wake up
resenting me, unsure why.

Now I'm in my son's dream.
Abe Lincoln's in here, tallest president,
along with Rich, tallest guy in church,
and football legend William "The Refrigerator" Perry.
My son stands tall among them.
I'm the only one here who's not big and strong.
I've had to give up so many
of my own dreams in order to find myself
in theirs. I've had to un-become
so many versions of myself.
I've had to stop listening to the man
I hoped to become, whispering in my head.
In a corner of my son's room,
dust shimmers, and colorful rays
of sunshine peek through the curtains.
For a second, Father, looking at that dust,
I understand how You can love
something weak and temporary like me.

Tom C. Hunley is a professor in the MFA/BA Creative Writing programs at Western Kentucky University. He won the 2020 Rattle Chapbook Prize for *Adjusting To The Lights*. In March 2021, C&R Press will release *What Feels Like Love: New and Selected Poems*.

you learn something every day
Josh Stenberg

but on the seventh day the lord rested
and what did we do? eddied;
raised ticks, ate pecan pie
mulled post cards or

junkets to the puppets.
we didn't get our act together,
needless to say: what was needful,
were you and the northern

lights, who gigged on the other
side of cloud cover while

something intervened here. those who
know, know. those who don't know:
enjoy your remains.

Anyway, it emerged only
later that these excited atoms, blocked
by unionized moisture, forecast and
downcast, constituted the final

reprieve.

to the obverse man
Josh Stenberg

three times daily will they ring and leave
bitter melon, black tea. outside the
people of the last land mass,
passing back and forth like tokens

on the felt. and then you call and
we are not together. all this cult of
tech just for each to tell the other:
again nothing happened here.

move right along, folks. nothing
to see here. although? someone, no
better than they should be, slouches
in the wings, waiting for the crew to

clear the stage.

Josh Stenberg is a Vancouver, Canada-born poet, now living in Australia, where he teaches Chinese literature and theatre. He has published poems in *CV2, TAR, Queen's Quarterly, Dalhousie Review, Event, Estuaire, filling Station, Grain* and others.

By the Swimming Pool
Michael Keshigian

The women share a secret,
chattering,
until we enter their circle,
giggling,
when they think we can't see.
We ask them for a hint,
but they intentionally turn away

then smile delicately
from the corners of their mouths,
increasing our need to know.
Perhaps it was something
they did long ago,
consequences notwithstanding,
the memory possesses
a enduring fascination.
It might explain their camaraderie,
the way they rest their chins
on the curl of their fists,
stare at each other
with intense intrigue.
Tell us one story
or give us a clue.
Whisper a sentence
or even a word
that might carry
in the warm summer breeze
when you close your eyes
to remember.

Michael Keshigian had his fourteenth poetry collection, *What To Do With Intangibles*, recently released in January, 2020 by Cyberwit.net. He has been published in numerous national and international journals, recently including *Pudding Magazine, Sierra Nevada Review, Oyez Review, Bluepepper*, and has appeared as feature writer in twenty publications with 7 Pushcart Prize and 2 Best Of The Net nominations. He lives in New Hampshire. (michaelkeshigian.com)

Corona–Vorona Days-Ways

Sandeep Kumar Mishra

The humanity is caving in slow corona motion
I like a sea mice back to my hide-hole,
Set an alarm every morn, lay in bed to ignore it
I stay, for what seems like minutes but becomes hours
Week and weeks in hibernation, am I a little lonely bear?

Sometimes I feel homesick in my home and
think I'm put in a home jail for not having corona,
It feels like a creepy clown chasing me
or I am being cornered by zombies,
I work from green home but the world is in red zone

As I log on for socialising and switch on to remote voice
Are vectors we all or postcodes alike,
My body robots repeat eat, sleep and eat
Is breakfast still breakfast if I have it at 12 ?
Is dinner still dinner if I have cookies for tea?

Now this thing is non-fiction- health vs economy
The virus does not care
for the digits in your bank account
or your total assets or the GDP,
And even the fiction is dark, but there's still music

The relentless race of traffic and people
have been turned into marathon conscious breath,
Shopping has became tracking down others health,
Sanitizer in the pockets,wearing face masks
Sneezing is new way to attract attention,
Corona warriors on the front line,
but some people still curse and cry
I blink my eyes, focusing in on the horizon
as if concentration itself will transport me to another place,

Did I just see a butterfly land in that flower?
When kookaburras cackle flying over empty streets
When the crickets' chirp sounds alone,
Do they know what is happening to us?
Am I noticing more than I did before?

The lungs feel clear, birds have replaced planes,
We venue out of the house to the garden and back in again
it's made all of us hermits
The sky is blue now, or is it just me?
Now I understand less means more

Covid-19 is a hydra- headed challenger
to our modern modality to wake up
buying cheap tack from cheap labour,
I wonder why I feel a sense of guilt
when I see others suffering while I am not,
But I am now getting used to my pyjamas

Sandeep Kumar Mishra is an outsider artist, poet and lecturer in English Literature and political Science. He is the art instructor at Kishlaya Outsider Art Academy. He lives in Australia and has edited a collection of poems by various poets - *Pearls* (2002) and written a professional guide book -*How to be* (2016) and a collection of poems and art - *Feel My Heart* (2016).

At Vespers
Eugene Stevenson

At Vespers, there is the square,
brown & grey mosaic stone
set in to white concrete.
The ritual begins, the faithful kneel
with earth & sky in prayer,
to make their call upon eternity.

The voices are mute: the old.
The voices murmur: the young.
The voices rise high: the innocent.

Candles burn, lips press, hands knot.
Weakened legs walk away.
Prayers answered are mysteries of stone.
With the gift of steps, a world grown
small, the empty square, keeps
its calendar according to the moon.

Eugene Stevenson lives in Raleigh, North Carolina, and writes to make some semblance of order out of disorder, to make sense of the unthinkable, to make still photographs out of daily rushes. His poems have appeared in *Chicago Tribune Magazine, DASH Literary Journal, Dime Show Review, Gravel Literary Magazine, The Hudson Review, Icarus,* and *Swamp Ape Review.*

The Table
J.T. Whitehead

I own this table.
I put *everything* down on it.
When I work as an attorney, my notes are on it.
The transcript of evidence, from which I take those notes,
Is something I review, while sitting at it.
Many convictions rest on or lie on this table.
With my elbows.
I mean "conviction" in both senses of the word.

This happened, before I began working from home.
This was already so, even before we were forced to go
Inside.
Our selves.

And that work I do, it feeds me.
So, then, I put the food on my table.

I play cards by myself, now.
We no longer share chance, odds, or risk.
I shuffle the deck on my table.

I deal.

I write and revise my poems on this table.

What I owe is also on this table.
I pay my bills, my dues, on this, my table.

My mother once owned this table.
So she, and this, my table, begat and support my everyday life.

Now it has four legs under it.
And I have named them.
There is no first in importance.
There is no last in importance.
I name them in the time in which they were placed beneath it:

William.
Daniel.
Joseph.
Tara.

    (*My legs*)

J.T. Whitehead is a a six-time Pushcart Prize nominated poet, one time Pushcart nominated short story author and was the winner of the Margaret Randall Poetry Prize in 2015. His first collection, *The Table of the Elements,* (Broadkill River Press, 2015), was nominated for the National Book Award. He lives in Indianapolis.

unbidden
Elizabeth Kidwell

I had no poems inside of me today,
Or so I thought, until they began to pour recklessly
And unbidden from my secret well of words.

Oozing through any small opening they found
In my mind, the letters began to tramp with black, muddy feet
Across a pure, blank page of expectant paper.

Impossible to stop them from charging forth with
Message and meaning, I surrendered to the crush of words
Giving voice to their insistent whisperings in the hushed silence.

Eager to exist, lines marched out in formation, established
Perfect rows marked with brevity and punctuation,
And then stood at attention in stanzas, waiting to be inspected.

Will they pass the muster of a general reader who expects
Meaning, perfection, polish, and shine? Or will this
Single poetic platoon be promoted to the higher rank of verse?

Once read, this rebel word song is no longer mine.
It will bugle on its own like a reveille at first light
To awaken sleeping minds and summon thought.

A native of Los Angeles, **Elizabeth Kidwell** grew up in the San Francisco Bay Area before returning to Los Angeles to attend college. Afterwards, she taught writing and literature at the secondary level for 5 years in Los Angeles and Ventura before moving to Indianapolis in 1974, where she continued her career in teaching and supervising for the next 40 years. She has been writing poetry for over 60 years, and while in college, she won the prestigious Cabrini Poetry Contest and an honorable mention in poetry from the *Atlantic Monthly Magazine.* Elizabeth Kidwell is also the author of a recently published book titled *Wounded Wings, A Lesbian Journey of Love and Loss*, recently published by Chatter House Press of Indianapolis, currently available on Amazon.com. The book contains 27 original poems, one in each chapter.

Mothballs
Karen L. George

Mothballs

Naphthalene or sometimes camphor.

What a neighbor laid to thwart cats from flowerbeds. What my sister hid to rid her car of ants. The sackful Grandma hung to repel moths. The scent drenched her coats—the smell of age—but cordial, clean like isopropyl alcohol.

Every fall, a coworker wore sweaters reeking mothballs.

Every time I pass the company garage, that funk pricks my nose, and I wonder again why he jumped.

Karen L. George lives in Kentucky and is author of five chapbooks, and two poetry collections from Dos Madres Press: *Swim Your Way Back* (2014) and *A Map and One Year* (2018). Her work has appeared in *Adirondack Review, Valparaiso Poetry Review, South Dakota Review, Naugatuck River Review,* and *SWWIM*. Karen reviews poetry at Poetry Matters: http://readwritepoetry.blogspot.com/, and is co-founder and fiction editor of the online journal, *Waypoints*: http://www.waypointsmag.com/. Visit her website at: https://karenlgeorge.blogspot.com/.

Sacred Ground

Mary Sexson

I could not find the right way to tell the priest what he needed to do. Ruth, he said, you can't ask me to do this. You know it isn't allowed. No suicides buried on holy ground. I wept at his feet, not for the drama, but for the sorrow of it: you alone in your car with a gun, our fruitless search for you, where? We didn't know which lonely country road you'd pulled off on. We couldn't see past the fields of corn and soybeans. There was nowhere to let your tired, broken mind rest. No blessed earth to receive you back, take you from my arms, again, and lay you down. I could bear it, I could hold myself straight up and hand you over to the fine dark loamy soil if I knew you would be safe there, next to your cousin, not far from our people, their simple graves spread out around the family marker. I needed the priest to do the right thing now, to back away from the strict rules he ministered this parish with and just be human, be Jesus, be the man who washed the feet of sinners. You can be the sinner he redeems. I will prostrate myself at his feet, I will wail like Mary when she looked upon her son.

Mary Sexson is the author of *103 in the Light, Selected Poems 1996-2000 (Restoration Press)*, and co-author of *Company of Women, New and Selected Poems* (Chatter House Press). Her poetry has appeared in *The Flying Island, Tipton Poetry Journal, Hoosier Lit, New Verse News*, and others, and several anthologies, including *Reckless Writing* (2013), *A Few Good Words* (2013), *The Best of Flying Island* (2015), and *Words and Other Wild Things* (2016). Her newest work is in *The Flying Island* (2019). She was a part of the Da Vinci Pursuit, a poetry project at Prophetstown State Park. Find her at **Poetry Sisters**, on Facebook.

Infinity Pool
Fred D. White

I keep swimming
toward an ending, but
there is no ending, except
that there most assuredly is
an ending or else I will plunge
to my death; but it is concealed by
the pool itself—by the water. Even so,
I swim toward it, getting ever closer to the
perceptually invisible, nonexistent terminus, the
ending I assume must be there in the form of a sub-
surface trough into which the water falls, and from which
it is returned—ending as beginning: a deep moral lesson à la
Ecclesiastes. The waters that carry us through life likewise fall
into an invisible trough while we smack against the limitations of
our being. "Whom do they think they're kidding with this infinity-pool
illusion," you might ask. "Why, everyone who stands awestruck before an
infinity pool, its water made to look inseparable from the ocean beyond, from
the earth itself. "Who are *they*, you ask." I Shrug "The designers, most likely, or
God himself, master of illusions."

Fred D. White's poems have appeared in *Allegro Poetry Journal, The Cape Rock, Rattle, South Carolina Review*, etc. He lives in Folsom, California.

Review: *Library of My Hands* by Joseph Heithaus

Reviewed by Joyce Brinkman

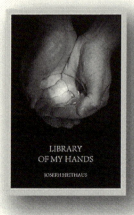

Title: **Library of My Hands**

Author: **Joseph Heithaus**

Publication Date: **June 14, 2020**
Publisher: **Dos Madres Press**

You have to be in the right mood to read *Library of My Hands*. I say that because if you are not in the right mood to read this book you will miss so much. What is the right mood? It should not be a casual read even though a casual read delights with enjoyable, enchanting sounds, but when you read it casually it's easy to be caught up in the beauty of its language while missing the depth of its observations and the very personal stories being told.

These poems don't scream this is my pain, my joy, my life. They don't insist this poem is about the poet. But when you read one with openness you discern its humanness and feel connection with both the poem's subject and the poet. He never hesitates to exude an honest and human response to whatever the myriad of things he encounters in the world. Each time he is struck with wonder, or fear, or excitement, or dread he wraps that encounter in inviting, informative and melodic words. Heithaus' poetic curiosity explores both the living world, such as in many of his nature inspired poems, like "Queen Anne's Lace."

in winter has thin brown arms

> *lifted like a ballerina's arms*
> *or your own arms when you*
> *offer up your grief*
> *or catch a toddler out of the air, chest open, head tilted*
> *up, fingers spread.*
> *Her arms catch the snow now lit like light itself,*
> *little ephemeral stars above the crooked crust of ice*

and even totally inanimate things such as in "Ode to A", which opens the book and brings new meaning to knowing the alphabet. He muses over words like *Forlorn* of which he writes,

> *I don't think there's a sadder word,*
>   *the way it droops and rhymes*

That then leads to human apprehension with

> *which so often leads*
> *to looking*
> *back*
> *forlornly*
> *at what might have been,*
> *or forward*
> *at the murky future*
> *split in two,*

He also acknowledges the reader and tries to help them explore their human misgivings such as in "Loss" with

> *Think*
> *of a jar of air and how*
> *it matches the feeling you have in your chest,*
> *all that emptiness clogging*
> *your throat, how you*
> *can't explain what they leave*
> *behind inside you,*
> *how the mouth can't*
> *hold them in,*

Sounding great makes poetry a joy: bringing the reader more in touch with their own humanity makes poetry invaluable.

This is not a one-time-read book. Heithaus and Dos Madres Press have both done a nice job presenting these poems in wonderfully thematic sections where several poems reside perfectly matched for an in depth dive into thoughtful exploration of the section's title. Each section is perfectly suited for a one-day read and contemplation.

In the spirit of full disclosure, I must say the first poem in the section Wish You Were Here resulted from a prompt for the workshop group Joe Heithaus and I belonged to when we were working on the books the group wrote as the Airpoets. As such it has to be my favorite poem in the book. There are however an abundance of poems to content for the honor of your favorite as you open this library stocked with shelves full of poetic handiwork.

Joseph (Joe) Heithaus, the youngest of six children, was born in South Bend, Indiana in 1962. *Poison Sonnets*, his first book, poems from which won the Discovery/The Nation Prize, explores through the sonnet form the language and chemistry of botany, the nature of poison, and its corollary—medicine. But the core of Joe's work is in his attention to the details of the world around him. *Library of My Hands* collects his poetic meditations on light, on family, and on language itself. While both his parents have passed away, they haunt the pages of this book and are central to his world view of wonder and gratitude. His mother and father, each raised in large families that had sacrificed to survive the Great Depression, told stories less about their hardships and more about the modest pleasures of ice cream, canned pineapple, and Sunday drives. His father's career with Chevrolet took their family from South Bend to Cincinnati, Ohio; Richmond, Virginia; and Syracuse, New York, where Joe finished high school before attending the State University of New York at Albany. After working in New York City he circled back to the Hoosier State to get his Ph.D. in American literature and his M.F.A. in poetry from Indiana University. In 1996, he began teaching at DePauw University in Greencastle, Indiana where he and his wife have raised their four children. His poetry and prose have appeared in many journals and anthologies including *Poetry, The Southern Review, Southwest Review, African American Review,* and *The New York Times.* You can also find Joe's poem "Indiana Flight" etched into a stained-glass window in concourse B of the Indianapolis International Airport and the poem "What Grows Here" on a barn beside West County Road 125 South just west of Greencastle.

Joyce Brinkman, Indiana Poet Laureate 2002-2008, believes in poetry as public art. She creates public poetry projects involving her poetry and the poetry of others. Collaborations with visual artists using her poetry for permanent installations include her words in a twenty- five foot stained glass window by British glass artist Martin Donlin at the Indianapolis International Airport, in lighted glass by Arlon Bayliss at the Indianapolis-Marion County Central Library and on a wall with local El Salvadoran artists in the town square of Quezaltepeque, El Salvador.

Her printed works include two chapbooks, " *Tiempo Español*, and *Nine Poems In Form Nine*, and two collaborative books, *Rivers, Rails and Runways*, and *Airmail from the Airpoets* from San Francisco Bay Press, with fellow "airpoets" Ruthelen Burns, Joe Heithaus, and Norbert Krapf.

Her latest books include the multinational, multilingual book *Seasons of Sharing A Kasen Renku Collaboration, from Leapfrog Press, Urban Voices: 51 Poems from 51 American Poets* from San Francisco Bay Press, which she co-edited with Carolyn Kreiter-Foronda and *Elizabeth Barrett Browning Illuminated by the Message* from ACTA Publications. Joyce organized the collaborative poems for the Indiana Bicentennial Legacy Book *Mapping the Muse* from Brick Street Poetry. She recently completed a public art project in Martinsville, Indiana, featuring poetry she wrote inspired by the life and words of UCLA basketball coach and Hoosier native John Wooden. She is a graduate of Hanover College. Joyce divides her time between Zionsville, Indiana, with her husband and a cantankerous cat.

Editor

Barry Harris is editor of the *Tipton Poetry Journal* and three anthologies by Brick Street Poetry: *Mapping the Muse: A Bicentennial Look at Indiana Poetry; Words and Other Wild Things* and *Cowboys & Cocktails:Poems from the True Grit Saloon.* He has published one poetry collection, *Something At The Center*.

Married and father of two grown sons, Barry Barry lives in Brownsburg, Indiana and is retired from Eli Lilly and Company.

He graduated a long time ago with a major in English from Ball State University.

His poetry has appeared in *Kentucky Review, Valparaiso Poetry Review, Grey Sparrow, Silk Road Review, Saint Ann's Review, Boston Literary Magazine, Night Train, Silver Birch Press, Flying Island, Awaken Consciousness, Writers' Bloc,* and *Red-Headed Stepchild.* One of his poems was on display at the National Museum of Sport and another is painted on a barn in Boone County, Indiana as part of Brick Street Poetry's Word Hunger public art project. His poems are also included in these anthologies: *From the Edge of the Prairie; Motif 3: All the Livelong Day;* and *Twin Muses: Art and Poetry.*

He graduated a long time ago with a major in English from Ball State University.

Contributor Biographies

M. Ait Ali is 28 years old, living in Agadir, Morocco and has works published in *Silly Linguistics, Nebula Adnauseum Magazine, Alien Buddha Press, Rogue Wolf Press, Spillwords*, and *A dove for peace* anthology.

Gilbert Allen's most recent collection of poems is *Catma*, from Measure Press. His book of linked stories, *The Final Days of Great American Shopping*, was published by University of South Carolina Press in 2016. A frequent contributor to TPJ, he is a member of the South Carolina Academy of Authors and the Bennette E. Geer Professor of Literature Emeritus at Furman University.

David M. Alper is a high school AP English teacher in New York City, residing in Manhattan. His work has appeared in *Thirty West Publishing House, OPEN: Journal of Arts & Letters, Glassworks Magazine*, and elsewhere.

Daniel Blackston is a professional writer and musician who lives and works in Springfield, Illinois.

Ann Boaden is an Illinois native. After earning her master's and doctoral degrees in English from The University of Chicago, she returned to teach at her undergraduate college, Augustana (Illinois). Work has appeared in *South Dakota Review, Big Muddy, Christmas on the Great Plains* (University of Iowa Press), *The Penwood Review, ACM (Another Chicago Magazine), Sediments, The Windhover*, and *Ginosko*, among other publications.

D.C. Buschmann is a retired editor and reading specialist. Her poem, "Death Comes for a Friend," was the Editor's Choice in *Poetry Quarterly*, Winter 2018. She has been published in the US, the UK, Australia, Iraq, and India, including Kurt Vonnegut Museum and Library's *So it Goes Literary Journal, Flying Island, The Adirondack Review, San Pedro River Review, Better Than Starbucks, Rat's Ass Review, Nerve Cowboy*, and elsewhere. She lives in Carmel, Indiana with husband Nick and miniature schnauzers Cupcake and Coco. Her first full collection of poetry will be published in 2020.

Joan Colby has published widely in journals such as *Poetry, Atlanta Review, South Dakota Review, Gargoyle, Pinyon, Little Patuxent Review, Spillway, Midwestern Gothic* and others. Awards include two Illinois Arts Council Literary Awards and an Illinois Arts Council Fellowship in Literature. She has published 21 books including *Selected Poems* from FutureCycle Press which received the 2013 FutureCycle Prize and *Ribcage* from Glass Lyre Press which has been awarded the 2015 Kithara Book Prize. Three of her poems have been featured on *Verse Daily* and another is among the winners of the 2016 Atlanta Review International Poetry Contest. Her newest books are *Carnival* from FutureCycle Press, *The Seven Heavenly Virtues* from Kelsay Books and *Her Heartsongs* from Presa Press.. Colby is a senior editor of FutureCycle Press and an associate editor of *Good Works Review*. Website: www.joancolby.com. Facebook: Joan Colby. Twitter: poetjm.

William Doreski lives in New Hampshire. His work has appeared in various journals and in several collections, most recently *Train to Providence*, a collaboration with photographer Rodger Kingston.

Michael Estabrook has been publishing his poetry in the small press since the 1980s. He has published over 20 collections, a recent one being *The Poet's Curse, A Miscellany* (The Poetry Box, 2019). He lives in Massachusetts.

Samantha Fain is an MFA candidate at Bowling Green State University. She studied creative writing at Franklin College. Her work has appeared in The *Indianapolis Review, SWWIM, Utterance*, and others. She tweets at @samcanliftacar.

David Flynn was born in the textile mill company town of Bemis, Tennessee. His jobs have included newspaper reporter, magazine editor and university teacher. He has five degrees and is both a Fulbright Senior Scholar and a Fulbright Senior Specialist with a recent grant in Indonesia. His literary publications total more than 220. Among the eight writing residencies he has been awarded are five at the Wurlitzer Foundation in Taos, New Mexico, and stays in Ireland and Israel. He spent a year in Japan as a member of the Japan Exchange and Teaching program. He currently lives in Nashville, Tennessee.

Karen L. George lives in Kentucky and is author of five chapbooks, and two poetry collections from Dos Madres Press: *Swim Your Way Back* (2014) and *A Map and One Year* (2018). Her work has appeared in *Adirondack Review, Valparaiso Poetry Review, South Dakota Review, Naugatuck River Review,* and *SWWIM*. Karen reviews poetry at Poetry Matters: http://readwritepoetry.blogspot.com/, and is co-founder and fiction editor of the online journal, *Waypoints*: http://www.waypointsmag.com/. Visit her website at: https://karenlgeorge.blogspot.com/.

Charles Grosel is an editor, writer, and poet living in Arizona. He has published stories in *Western Humanities Review, Fiction Southeast, Red Cedar Review, Water-Stone,* and *The MacGuffin* and poems *in Slate, The Threepenny Review, Poet Lore, Cream City Review* and *Harpur Palate,* among others. *The Sound of Rain Without Water*, a chapbook of poems, is coming out in the next year.

Tim Hawkins' short fiction and poetry can be found in many print and online magazines and anthologies. He has published a poetry collection, *Wanderings at Deadline* (Aldrich Press, 2012), a poetry chapbook, *Jeremiad Johnson* (In Case of Emergency Press, 2019), and a story and poetry chapbook*, Synchronized Swimmers* (KYSO Flash Press, 2019). His second full-length poetry collection, *West of the Backstory*, is forthcoming in late 2020 from Fernwood Press. Tim lives in Michigan. Find out more at his website: www.timhawkinspoetry.com.

Tom C. Hunley is a professor in the MFA/BA Creative Writing programs at Western Kentucky University. He won the 2020 Rattle Chapbook Prize for *Adjusting To The Lights*. In March 2021, C&R Press will release *What Feels Like Love: New and Selected Poems*.

Mihika Jain lives in India. She is a passionate writer and poet who has had her work published on various platforms. Her other interests include music, art, and politics.

Kit Kennedy is a queer elder living in Walnut Creek, California. She has published 7 collections including "while eating oysters" (CLWN WR BKS, Brooklyn, NY). Work has appeared in *Tipton Poetry Journal, Great Weather for Media, First Literary Review-East, Gyroscope, Glass*, among others. She serves as Poet in Residence of SF Bay Times and Resident Poet at Ebenezer Lutheran "herchurch." Please visit: http://poetrybites.blogspot.com.

Michael Keshigian had his fourteenth poetry collection, *What To Do With Intangibles*, recently released in January, 2020 by Cyberwit.net. He has been published in numerous national and international journals, recently including *Pudding Magazine, Sierra Nevada Review, Oyez Review, Bluepepper*, and has appeared as feature writer in twenty publications with 7 Pushcart Prize and 2 Best Of The Net nominations. He lives in New Hampshire. (michaelkeshigian.com)

A native of Los Angeles, **Elizabeth Kidwell** grew up in the San Francisco Bay Area before returning to Los Angeles to attend college. Afterwards, she taught writing and literature at the secondary level for 5 years in Los Angeles and Ventura before moving to Indianapolis in 1974, where she continued her career in teaching and supervising for the next 40 years. She has been writing poetry for over 60 years, and while in college, she won the prestigious Cabrini Poetry Contest and an honorable mention in poetry from the *Atlantic Monthly Magazine*. Elizabeth Kidwell is also the author of a recently published book titled *Wounded Wings, A Lesbian Journey of Love and Loss*, recently published by Chatter House Press of Indianapolis, currently available on Amazon.com. The book contains 27 original poems, one in each chapter.

Richard Krohn lived much of his life up and down the East Coast, north and south, but with several years at various times in the Midwest and also in Central America. He presently teaches Economics and Spanish at Moravian College in Bethlehem, Pennsylvania. In recent years his poetry has appeared in *Poet Lore, Southern Poetry Review, Arts & Letters, Tar River,* and *Rattle*, among many others.

Dr. Ryan David Leack teaches writing and rhetoric at the University of Southern California. He's published poetry in *Chiron Review, Pif, and Westwind*, among other journals, and also served as Editor-in-Chief of *Pomona Valley Review* for seven years.

Brooke Dwojak Lehmann holds a B.S.in Chemical Engineering from Purdue University. Poetry has been published by *Black Fox Literary Magazine* and *Parentheses*. Brooke lives in Seattle where she freelances as a fashion model and consultant.

Bruce Levine a 2019 Pushcart Prize Poetry Nominee, has spent his life as a writer of fiction and poetry and as a music and theatre professional. Over 300 of his works are published in over 25 on-line journals including *Ariel Chart, Friday Flash Fiction, Literary Yard;* over 30 print books including *Poetry Quarterly, Haiku Journal, Dual Coast Magazine*, and his shows have been produced in New York and around the country. Six eBooks are available from Amazon.com. His work is dedicated to the loving memory of his late wife, Lydia Franklin. He lives in New York with his dog, Daisy. Visit him at www.brucelevine.com.

Christian Lozada is the product of an immigrant Filipino and Daughter of the American Revolution and has co-written the poetry book *Leave with More Than You Came With*, published by Arroyo Secco Press and a photographic history book *Hawaiians in Los Angeles*. Poetry has been anthologized in *Gutters and Alleyways: Poems on Poverty*, (Cadence Collective), and his poems and stories have appeared in *Hawaii Pacific Review* (forthcoming), *Dryland: A Literary Journal, A&U Magazine, Spot Literary Journal, Blue Collar Review* and various other journals. Christian has hosted the Read on till Morning literary series and Harbor College Poetry Night, and invited to read or speak at the Autry Museum, the Twin Towers Correctional Facility, and other places throughout Southern California.

Doris Lynch lives in Bloomington, Indiana and has recent work in *Flying Island, Frogpond, Modern Haiku, Contemporary Haibun Online, Drifting Sands Haibun* and in the anthologies: *Cowboys & Cocktails: Poetry from the True Grit Saloon* (Brick Street Poetry Inc., 2019), *Red River book of Haibun* (Red River Press, New Delhi, India, 2019), and *Another Trip Around the Sun: 365 Days of Haiku for Children Young and Old*, (Brooks Books, 2019).

R. Nikolas Macioci earned a PhD from The Ohio State University. OCTELA, the Ohio Council of Teachers of English, named Nik Macioci the best secondary English teacher in the state of Ohio. Nik is the author of two chapbooks as well as six books: More than two hundred of his poems have been published here and abroad, including *The Society of Classic Poets Journal, Chiron, The Comstock Review, Concho River Review*, and *Blue Unicorn*. Forthcoming books are *Rough* and *Why Dance?*

Jennifer McClellan is an Evansville, Indiana poet based poet. She has written poetry since she was a teenager, though this is her first time appearing in a literary journal. She believes poetry and music are the heart of human connection and is thrilled to share her writing.

Karla Linn Merrifield has had 800+ poems appear in dozens of journals and anthologies. She has 14 books to her credit. Following her 2018 *Psyche's Scroll* (Poetry Box Select) is the 2019 full-length *Athabaskan Fractal: Poems of the Far North* from Cirque Press. She is currently at work on a poetry collection, *My Body the Guitar*, inspired by famous guitarists and their guitars to be published by Before Your Quiet Eyes Holograph Series (Rochester, New York) in late 2021.

Sandeep Kumar Mishra is an outsider artist, poet and lecturer in English Literature and political Science. He is the art instructor at Kishlaya Outsider Art Academy. He lives in Australia and has edited a collection of poems by various poets - *Pearls* (2002) and written a professional guide book -*How to be* (2016) and a collection of poems and art - *Feel My Heart* (2016).

Lorne Mook grew up on a farm in northwest Pennsylvania and now lives in Upland, Indiana, where he is Associate Professor of English at Taylor University. In 2011 he published the first English translation of Rainer Maria Rilke's third book of poems, *Dream-Crowned*. His translations have also appeared *in AGNI, Poetry International, Literary Imagination*, and other journals. A collection of his own poems, *Travelers Without Maps*, was published in 2002.

Janet Reed earned a Master's degree in English Literature from Pittsburg State University in Kansas. She currently teaches writing and literature at Crowder College in Missouri. She has work published in multiple journals with more forthcoming.

Maree Reedman lives in Brisbane, Australia with one husband, two cockatiels, and five ukuleles. Her poetry has appeared or is forthcoming in Australia and the United States in *The Chiron Review, StylusLit, Unbroken, Hecate*, and other places. Her poetry has won awards in The Ipswich Poetry Feast. She loves poetry that tells a good story.

Timthy Robbins has been teaching English as a Second Language for 28 years. His poems have appeared in *Main Street Rag, Off The Coast, Bayou Magazine, Slant, Tipton Poetry Journal, Cholla Needles* and many others. He has published three volumes of poetry: *Three New Poets* (Hanging Loose Press), *Denny's Arbor Vitae* (Adelaide Books) and *Carrying Bodies* (Main Street Rag Press). He lives in Wisconsin with his husband of 22 years.

Laura Saint Martin is a writer of fiction and poetry, with several short pieces published in online journals and print anthologies. She lives in Rancho Cucamonga, California.

Mary Sexson is the author of *103 in the Light, Selected Poems 1996-2000 (Restoration Press)*, and co-author of *Company of Women, New and Selected Poems* (Chatter House Press). Her poetry has appeared in *The Flying Island, Tipton Poetry Journal, Hoosier Lit, New Verse News*, and others, and several anthologies, including *Reckless Writing* (2013), *A Few Good Words* (2013), *The Best of Flying Island* (2015), and *Words and Other Wild Things* (2016). Her newest work is in *The Flying Island* (2019). She was a part of the Da Vinci Pursuit, a poetry project at Prophetstown State Park. Find her at **Poetry Sisters**, on Facebook.

David Spicer lives in Memphis and has published poems in *The American Poetry Review, CircleStreet, Gargoyle, Moria, Oyster River Pages, Ploughshares, Remington Review, Santa Clara Review, The Sheepshead Review, Steam Ticket, Synaeresis, Third Wednesday*, and elsewhere. Nominated for a Best of the Net three times and a Pushcart twice, he is author of six chapbooks, the latest being *Tribe of Two* (Seven CirclePress). His latest full-length collections, *American Maniac* (Hekate Publishing) and *Confessional* (Cyberwit.net), are now available. His website is www.davidspicer76.com.

Josh Stenberg is a Vancouver, Canada-born poet, now living in Australia, where he teaches Chinese literature and theatre. He has published poems in *CV2, TAR, Queen's Quarterly, Dalhousie Review, Event, Estuaire, filling Station, Grain* and others.

Shelby Stephenson was North Carolina's poet laureate 2015-18 and editor of *Pembroke Magazine* for 32 years. His current book of poems: *Slavery and Freedom on Paul's Hill*.

Eugene Stevenson lives in Raleigh, North Carolina, and writes to make some semblance of order out of disorder, to make sense of the unthinkable, to make still photographs out of daily rushes. His poems have appeared in *Chicago Tribune Magazine, DASH Literary Journal, Dime Show Review, Gravel Literary Magazine, The Hudson Review, Icarus*, and *Swamp Ape Review*.

Denise Thompson-Slaughter is a writer living in Western New York. Her published work includes two books of poetry (*Sixty-ish: Full Circle,* Spirited Muse Press, 2017; and *Elemental,* Plain View Press, 2010), a novella (*Mystery Gifts,* Spirited Muse Press, 2018), a couple of short stories, and a handful of brief memoir pieces, the most recent of which was published in the May issue of *Dash Literary Journal.*

The poet laureate of Grand Rapids, Michigan from 2007-2010, **Rodney Torreson** is the author of four books. A fifth book of poems, co-authored with Russell Thorburn and forthcoming from Finishing Line Press, is entitled *The Jukebox Was the Jury of their Love.* His poems have recently appeared in *Artful Dodge, Miramar, Poet Lore, Tar River Poetry, Third Coast,* and *Tipton Poetry Journal.*

Gene Twaronite is a Tucson poet and the author of nine books, including collections of poetry, short stories and essays as well as two juvenile fantasy novels. His latest book is *My Life as a Sperm: Essays from the Absurd Side.* Follow more of his writing @thetwaronitezone.com.

Sheila Wellehan's poetry is featured in *Menacing Hedge, Rust + Moth, Thimble Literary Magazine, Tinderbox Poetry Journal, Whale Road Review,* and many other journals and anthologies. She lives in Cape Elizabeth, Maine. Visit her online at www.sheilawellehan.com.

Kelly Whiddon lives in Georgia and has published in *Crab Orchard Review, Southeast Review, Poetry International, Southern Poetry Review,* and *Meridian,* among others. Her book, *The House Began to Pitch* (Mercer UP), was honored with the Adrienne Bond Poetry Award, and she has served as associate editor of *Apalachee Review* and is on the staff of *International Quarterly.* You can find more info at www.kellywhiddon.com.

Fred D. White's poems have appeared in *Allegro Poetry Journal, The Cape Rock, Rattle, South Carolina Review,* etc. He lives in Folsom, California.

J.T. Whitehead is a a six-time Pushcart Prize nominated poet, one time Pushcart nominated short story author and was the winner of the Margaret Randall Poetry Prize in 2015. His first collection, *The Table of the Elements,* (Broadkill River Press, 2015), was nominated for the National Book Award. He lives in Indianapolis.

Anne Whitehouse is the author of six poetry collections, most recently *Meteor Shower* (Dos Madres Press, 2016). She has also written a novel, *Fall Love,* which is now available in Spanish translation as *Amigos y amantes* by Compton Press. Recent honors include 2018 Prize Americana for Prose, 2017 Adelaide Literary Award in Fiction, 2016 Songs of Eretz Poetry Prize, 2016 Common Good Books' Poems of Gratitude Contest, 2016 RhymeOn! Poetry Prize, 2016 F. Scott and Zelda Fitzgerald Museum Poetry Prize. She lives in New York City. www.annewhitehouse.com

Made in the USA
Middletown, DE
28 August 2020